4

SPORTING 🏆 HEROES

SERENA WILLIAMS

ROY APPS

ILLUSTRATED BY ALESSANDRO VALDRIGHI

Franklin Watts
Published in paperback in Great Britain in 2018
by The Watts Publishing Group

Text © Roy Apps 2018
Illustrations © Watts Publishing Group 2018
Illustrator: Alessandro Valdrighi
Cover design by Peter Scoulding
Executive Editor: Adrian Cole

*The statistics in this book were correct at the time
of printing, but because of the nature of the sport,
it cannot be guaranteed that they are now accurate.*

HB ISBN 978 1 4451 5338 4
PB ISBN 978 1 4451 5341 4
Library ebook ISBN 978 1 4451 5340 7

1 3 5 7 9 10 8 6 4 2

Printed in China

Franklin Watts
An imprint of
Hachette Children's Group
Part of The Watts Publishing Group
Carmelite House
50 Victoria Embankment
London EC4Y 0DZ

An Hachette UK Company
www.hachette.co.uk

www.franklinwatts.co.uk

*Serena's family called her Meeka, instead of Serena Jameka

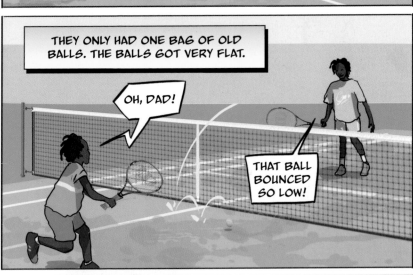

CHAPTER TWO
LITTLE SISTER

Serena was just three years old when she first picked up a tennis racket. By the time she was five she was playing with her sister Venus, who was just fifteen months older than she was. By now their mum had joined their dad in coaching them. Their three older sisters played tennis, too, but they all had other interests.

As they got older, people at competitions began to take notice of the two young Williams girls. Well, they took notice of Venus; she was tall and athletic. Serena was small for her age.

'It's like I'm invisible!' she told her eldest sister, Tunde, with a sigh.

'Take no notice, Meeka,' Tunde said. 'Your time will come. Believe me.'

'Yes, but how long until my time comes?' thought Serena. Every weekend, Venus went to a tennis tournament to play a proper match. Serena used to tag along to watch.

One day, Serena decided she'd had enough of just watching. She wandered over to the organisers' tent.

SERENA'S DAD WASN'T MAD. HE WAS HAPPY!

MEEKA! YOU PLAYED GREAT! YOU WON!'

HEY, HOW ABOUT THAT! BOTH OF OUR GIRLS – WINNERS!

CHAPTER THREE
NOT-SO-LITTLE SISTER

One day, when she was nine, Serena's father came home from work and spoke to her and her sisters.

'I've done pretty well coaching Venus and Serena,' he said, 'but it's time I had some professional help.'

The girls' mum agreed. 'You're right. Venus is a better player than you are, now.'

So the family packed everything in their VW microbus and moved to Florida. There, Serena and Venus attended a tennis academy run by a highly-respected coach named Rick Macci.

By now Venus was a star. As a junior,

she never lost a match. She was interviewed for magazines and TV. Sometimes, Serena would get a mention in an article:

Venus' younger sister, Serena plays tennis, too.

But the rest of the time, Serena was very much in the background.

In 1995, when she was fourteen, Serena became old enough to become a professional tennis player. She lost her first tournament match 6—1, 6—1. Feeling downhearted, it was two years before she played another tournament match.

The first three tournaments she played in 1997 she lost in the qualifying round. But people watching the Williams sisters play noticed something:

'Hey, the little sister isn't so little any more.'

Serena had put on a growth spurt. She still wasn't quite as tall as Venus, but she didn't have to do so much scurrying about the court as she once had.

Things began to click. In the 1997 Ameritech Cup, and ranked 304th Serena beat two top seeds, Mary Pierce and Monica Seles. She finished the year ranked 99 in the world. She was only 16.

Serena began competing in the Grand Slam tournaments — the most important tournaments on the professional tennis circuit. In 1999, she won her first Grand Slam title, becoming the US Open

Champion. She had become only the
second African-American woman
to win a Grand Slam title.

Serena finished the year ranked 4th in the world, just one place behind her sister, Venus.

Things were going well for the Williams sisters. But not everybody was thrilled about their success. A few years before, the girls' father had withdrawn his daughters from a junior tournament after they had been the subject of racial abuse by the parents of some white girls. Serena didn't know it, but worse was to come...

CHAPTER FOUR
INDIAN WELLS

As two top-ranked tennis players, Serena and her sister were used to playing against each other in tournaments. By 2001, they'd played each other five times; Venus had won four of those matches, Serena one. That year they were both playing in the Indian Wells Masters tournament, which was held at Palm Springs in California.

They both did well in the early rounds. If they both won their quarter-final matches they would be playing each other in the semi-final. Serena won her quarter-final match easily enough, but Venus struggled in hers. Indian Wells is in the desert. It was unbearably hot and Venus went down with cramp.

She scraped through the match; but in trying to deal with her cramp she had hurt her knee, badly.

On the day of the semi-final against each other, Venus could hardly stand.

The tournament organisers should have made an official announcement explaining that Venus had withdrawn from the match because of injury, but for some reason they didn't.

The sell-out crowd, who had paid for tickets to see the Williams sisters fight it out in an epic semi-final battle had no idea that Venus was injured. They sat looking at an empty court, growing angrier by the minute.

'We want our money back!'

'It's a fix!'

Because of Venus' injury, Serena was now straight through to the final. The tournament organisers eventually made an announcement about Venus' injury, and Serena thought that would be that. She was wrong.

When she stepped onto the court for her finals match against the former Belgian Junior champion, Kim Clijsters, she was met with a roar of boos from the crowd.

'Cheat! Cheat! Cheat!'

As the match went on, the chanting got worse. Racist taunts were shouted out not just to Serena, but to her family, who were watching the match.

Serena tried to block out the sound, but she couldn't. She was close to tears. She lost the first set 6—4.
The boos turned to jeers. The racist chanting got worse. The organisers did nothing to try and stop the crowd's sickening behaviour.

'I can't go on,' Serena thought. 'I just can't!'

CHAPTER FIVE
THE SERENA SLAM

Serena was about to pick up her bag and walk off the court, when she looked up into the crowd towards her father. She remembered him telling her about the tennis player Althea Gibson. Her father had said she was the first African-American woman to win a Grand Slam title. She'd won the Australian Open, French Open, US Open and Wimbledon — twice — in the 1950s. Racial segregation in the US meant that Althea wasn't allowed to stay in hotels, and had spent the nights when she was playing tournaments sleeping in her car.

'What Althea suffered was far worse than this, and she didn't give up. Neither will I!' thought Serena.

Serena returned to the court for the second set. When play resumed, Kim Clijsters made a couple of unforced errors. Serena looked up across the net and saw that her opponent was upset. The racist chanting was affecting her game as well. To continuing catcalls from the crowd, Serena went on the win the match 4—6, 6—4, 6—2.

After a tournament win, the journey home was usually marked by singing and laughter. In the VW microbus on the way home from Indian Wells, the mood was sombre; everybody was in shock and nobody said a word.

It would be fourteen years before Serena entered the Indian Wells tournament again.

There was now a steely resolve about Serena's play. She powered through the French Open, the U.S. Open and Wimbledon, beating Venus in the finals of each tournament. Her dream of the 'Serena Slam' was in sight; there was just more Grand Slam tournament to win: the Australian Open.

Serena came through the early rounds easily enough, but when she reached the semi-finals, her nerves began to show. Her opponent was Kim Clijsters, who she had played in the final at Indian Wells. Serena and Kim took one set each, but then in the deciding set Serena folded completely. She found herself 1—5 down with two match points against her. Surely her dream was over?

But Serena had a habit of coming back from impossible positions. She kept a tennis 'match book' of phrases and words, which she wrote down to inspire and fire herself up to win. She remembered what she'd written in her match book earlier:

Just tell me it's out of reach. Come on. I'll prove U wrong!

It worked! Serena saved both match points. She went on to win five games in a row, and then the tie-break, to win the set and the match 4—6, 6—3, 7—5.

'I've always been a fighter,' she told the press.

In the final Serena beat — who else — her sister Venus to realise her dream of winning four Grand Slam titles in a row: her very own 'Serena Slam'.

She was on top of the world.

CHAPTER SIX
TRAGEDY

Professional tennis is a hard and demanding business. You need time to recover. Which was why, a few weeks after beating Venus to win the 2013 Wimbledon title, Serena was dancing the night away at a club in Los Angeles.

As she spun round on the dance floor, she felt something go in her knee.

She knew straight away that it was serious.

At the hospital, the doctor told her: 'You're going to need an operation.' She would be out of the professional tennis circuit for months. Then, one night while she was sleeping, Serena received a phone call…

For the next few months, life for Serena went by in a haze. Serena and her family found comfort in each other and in their faith.

Serena has never forgotten her big sister. You will often see her wearing orange when she is playing tennis. Orange was Tunde's favourite colour.

CHAPTER SEVEN
THE LONG ROAD BACK

Although Serena recovered well from her knee injury, she found it difficult to get back into the rhythm of playing professional tennis again.

The death of Tunde had a profound effect on her. Suddenly, hitting a ball around a tennis court didn't seem quite as important to her as it once had.

She made two trips to Africa. She visited the notorious 'slave castles' in Senegal on the West African coast, where Africans, Serena's ancestors amongst them, had been imprisoned by traders before being shipped as slaves to North America.

'I can't believe my own ancestors were

kept here and starved and tortured,'
she thought.

Serena also helped set up a school in
Ghana, and spent time playing tennis
with groups of village children.

She was still playing professional tennis,
but she was no longer number 1.
Her ability to win important matches
seemed to have deserted her. She began
to miss training sessions, and because
she missed training the level of her
fitness began to drop. A lower level
of fitness meant she was losing more
matches. At one point during 2006,
her world ranking slumped to an
all-time low of 139. It seemed as
if Serena Williams' career as a
professional tennis player was over.

At least that's what some commentators
reckoned: 'She's a bit of a has-been,'
they said. 'Out of shape.'

'She thinks she can make it back to the top? Some hope.'

Listening to these so-called experts writing her off started to kindle Serena's passion to be a winner again.

'Who do these people think they are?'

Serena wrote in her match book:

Tell me 'No' and I'll show U I can!
Go ahead, just tell me I can't win.
Just tell me 'No' and watch what happens.

Serena began training hard. It wasn't easy, but she fought her way through the early rounds of the 2007 Australian Open. She found herself in the final, where her opponent was the top seed, Maria Sharapova. The commentators still didn't rate her chances.

'Serena's had a great tournament,

but the ride is over. Maria will have
no trouble beating her.'

When Serena saw that on the TV, she
reached straight for her match book:

Just tell me 'No' and watch what happens.

'You'd better believe it!' she said
to herself.

Serena stormed through the first
set 6—1.

SERENA WON'T
BE ABLE TO KEEP
THAT PACE UP...

SHE CAN'T. SHE'S
OUT OF MATCH PRACTICE.

CHAPTER EIGHT
BACK ON TOP

By 2009, Serena was back to being number 1 in the world rankings. She and Venus had also done well in the doubles, where they were ranked third in the world.

In 2015, Serena won Wimbledon, completing her second 'Serena Slam'.

Serena defended her title at Wimbledon in 2016, equalling Steffi Graf's record of 22 Grand Slam wins. Later that year, with a 6–2, 6–3 victory over Yaroslava Shvedova at the 2016 US Open, she set a new Grand Slam record of 308 victories, to pass Roger Federer in the all-time list of matches won at major tennis tournaments. Serena was back on top!

SPORTING 🏆 HEROES

FACT FILE

Full name: Serena Jameka Williams

Childhood nickname: Meeka

Date of birth: 26th September 1981

Place of birth: Saginaw, Michigan, USA

Height: 1.75m (5ft 7in)

GLOSSARY

ancestors — people in the past from whom we are descended

cramp — painful, uncontrollable tightening of a muscle

drive-by shooting — when someone fires a gun from a moving vehicle, typically at pedestrians or other vehicles

Grand Slam — a set of major championships (majors) in the same year (in tennis: Australian Open, French Open, Wimbledon, US Open)

racist — showing discrimination or prejudice against people of other races

seeds — top positions in a competition, given to the best athletes based on recent performances

segregation — keeping some people, often of different races, apart from others

CAREER

Grand Slam Singles titles:

Australian Open	2003, 2005, 2007, 2009, 2010, 2015, 2017
French Open	2002, 2013, 2015
Wimbledon	2002, 2003, 2009, 2010, 2012, 2015, 2016
US Open	1999, 2002, 2008, 2012, 2013, 2014

Grand Slam Doubles titles (with Venus Williams):

Australian Open	2001, 2003, 2009, 2010
French Open	1999, 2010
Wimbledon	2000, 2002, 2008, 2009, 2012, 2016
US Open	1999, 2009

Charity work:

Serena is heavily involved in charity work. In 2008, she set up the Serena Williams Fund. Amongst other things, this charity runs a school in Kenya and offers University scholarships to disadvantaged students in the US. She has been an International Goodwill Ambassador with UNICEF since 2011 and has helped launch UNICEF's Schools for Asia campaign.

Languages:

Serena speaks English and French. At the 2016 French Open she gave her on-court interviews in French, delighting the home crowd.

Fashion:

Serena designs clothes and launched her own collection at the New York Fashion Week in 2015.

Miami Dolphins:

In August 2009, Williams and her sister Venus became minority owners of the American football club Miami Dolphins.

SPORTING 🏆 HEROES

It was scary. Lonely. On the streets
at night. There were noises everywhere.
Cars and taxis hooting, buses revving,
people calling out and shouting.

One night, while Fara was curled up
under the arches down by the river, an
old guy came and sat down beside her...
He looked hard at the football boots
Fara was clutching.

'Nice boots.
Do you play?'

Fara nodded.
'For Chelsea
Ladies...'

CONTINUE READING
FARA'S
AMAZING STORY IN...

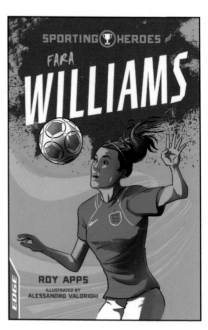

SPORTING 🏆 HEROES
FARA
WILLIAMS

ROY APPS
ILLUSTRATED BY
ALESSANDRO VALDRIGHI

EDGE